RESIDENTIAL

SPACES

OF THE WORLD

VOLUME 1

RESIDENTIAL

SPACES

OF THE WORLD

VOLUME 1

A PICTORIAL REVIEW OF RESIDENTIAL INTERIORS

ISBN 1 875498 23 0
© 1994
Images Australia Pty Ltd
Melbourne, Australia 1994
Printed in Hong Kong

Contents

Introduction

Introduction

The creation of residential spaces for individual clients can place architects/designers in a sometimes difficult but certainly always challenging position. They are obliged to tailor their own creative talent and training so as to provide designs, which while inspired by their own attitudes, imagination and experiences, meet the frequently heavy constraints of the client's brief.

Obviously, when creating a livable environment to suit the stated desires of an individual client, constraints like the budget, site, aspect, access etc., must be taken into account. More important though for the architect/designer of an individual home is to be able to blend these practical considerations with the use of light, space and materials, the essential elements of architecture, so as to develop a response which aspires to elevate the design, and in turn the client's own view of the resulting environment, beyond the ordinary.

My work as a recorder of these spaces has given me the opportunity to experience a wide variety of responses by architects/designers to their clients' needs, and often I am asked which of these I think might be the best. There is no right answer. Every space is crafted by the designer to reflect and inspire the lives of those who will inhabit it. The skill of the residential designer lies in the ability to create an environment which is, in a sense, more profound than the sum of its parts.

Housing represents the most direct interface between architecture and the public. It is the one form of architecture through which all humanity passes. That such a variety of responses can be produced to fulfil the fundamental need for human shelter is testimony to the talent and diversity of the architects and designers who pursue the challenge of creating residential spaces.

Tim Griffith

Living Spaces

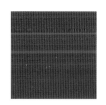

1

1&2
Baan Rimtai Saitarn
Mae-Rim Chiang Mai, Thailand
Architects 49 Limited
Photo credit: Architects 49

3 Sophia Court Apartment
Singapore
KNTA Architects
Photo credit: I.D. Magazine

2

2

1 Beckhard House
New York, USA
Herbert Beckhard, Architect
Photo credit: Nick Wheeler

2 & 3
Talma Building
Victoria, Australia
City of Melbourne,
Urban Design and Architecture Division
and Geyer Design Pty Ltd
Photo credit: City of Melbourne

3

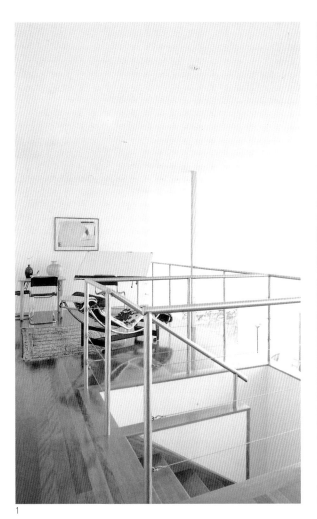

1

2

3

Previous
   Vacation House
   Quebec, Canada
   DuBose Associates, Inc., Architects
   Photo credit: Robert Benson

1 & 2
   Ocean House
   New South Wales, Australia
   Cox Architects
   Photo credit: Adrian Boddy

3 & 4
   Ocean House
   New South Wales, Australia
   Cox Architects
   Photo credit: Patrick Bingham-Hall

5 **Ocean House**
   New South Wales, Australia
   Cox Architects
   Photo credit: Adrian Boddy

4

5

Above & Opposite
Alderbrook Farm
Massachusetts, USA
Dean Tucker Shaw Inc
Photo credit: Steve Rosenthal

1

2

3

1&3
  Tomewin House
  Queensland, Australia
  Philip Follent Architects Pty Ltd
  in association with
  Denis Holland - Didec Design
  Photo credit: Dick Stringer

2&6
  Tomewin House
  Queensland, Australia
  Philip Follent Architects Pty Ltd
  in association with
  Denis Holland - Didec Design
  Photo credit: Jane Ulrick

4 **"The Townhouse"**
  Victoria, Australia
  Fooks Martin Sandow Pty Ltd
  Photo credit: Peter Sandow

5 **Foster Residence**
  Victoria, Australia
  Richardson Christoff Pty. Ltd. Architects
  Photo credit: Unknown

4

5

6

1 & 2
McMeckan Residence
Victoria, Australia
Fooks Martin Sandow Pty Ltd
Photo credit: Unknown

3-5
Dillon Residence
Dunedin, New Zealand
Interact Architectural & Design
Services Limited
Photo credit: Gary Van Der Mark

1

3

4

5

2

Opposite
Owner's Suite at the Royal
Hawaiian Hotel
Hawaii, USA
Projects International
Photo credit: Rothenborg Pacific

2 & 3
The Heritage on the Garden
Massachusetts, USA
The Architects Collaborative Inc.
Photo credit: Steve Rosenthal

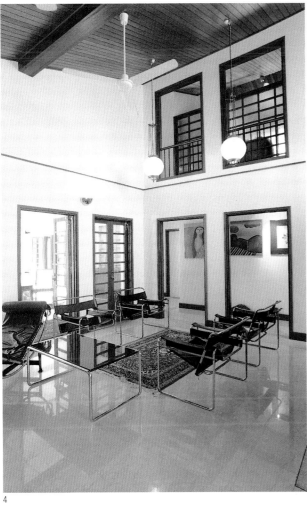

1 & 2
Yu Residence
Talayan Village, Philippines
G & W Architects & Associates
Photo credit: R RL Photography

3 Binondo Penthouse
Manila, Philippines
G & W Architects & Associates
Photo credit: R RL Photography

4 & 5
T House
Kuala Lumpur, Malaysia
Pakatan Reka Arkitek
Photo credit: KL NG Photography

6 Lawrence Residence
The Claymore, Singapore
Design Ideas International Group
Photo credit: Xiao Photos

4

5

6

1

1&2
Bollig Residence
Western Australia, Australia
Bollig Abbott Architects
Photo credit: Richard Worldendorp

3&4
St. Georges Road Residence
Victoria, Australia
Holgar & Holgar Architects
Photo credit: Michal Sikorski (Stockholm)

5 **Johnson Miller Residence**
Victoria, Australia
Bochsler and Partners Pty Ltd
Photo credit: Neil Lorimer

2

3

4

1

2

3

4

5

1 & 2
Srhoy Residence
Western Australia, Australia
Bollig Abbott Architects
Photo credit: Richard Worldendorp

3 Schwarz Residence
Victoria, Australia
Bochsler and Partners Pty Ltd
Photo credit: Neil Lorimer

4 M House
Petaling Jaya, Malaysia
Pakatan Reka Arkitek
Photo credit: KL NG Photography

5 Johnny Mak Residence
Hong Kong
Alice Lem Design
Photo credit: Unknown

6 McFarlane Residence
Victoria, Australia
Richardson Christoff Pty. Ltd. Architects
Photo credit: Max Deliopolous

6

1-4
House Jauhiainen
Espoo, Finland
Jauhiainen CJN Architects
Photo credit: Hannu Männynoksa

5 House addition and renovation
Connecticut, USA
DuBose Associates, Inc., Architects
in conjunction with Theurkauf & Co.
Photo credit: Robert Benson

2

1 House addition and renovation
Connecticut, USA
DuBose Associates, Inc., Architects
in conjunction with Theurkauf & Co.
Photo credit: Robert Benson

2 Pomeroy Residence
New York, USA
Lee Harris Pomeroy Associates/Architects
Photo credit: Paul Warchol

2

3

1&2
Manhattan Apartment, Trump Tower
New York, USA
Dorothy Draper & Co. Inc.
Photo credit: Feliciano

3&4
Residence at Makepeace
Singapore
Timur Designs
Photo credit: Tim Nolan

4

Opposite and 1&2
Residence at Makepeace
Singapore
Timur Designs
Photo credit: Tim Nolan

1

1

1&2
Schnyder House
Kuala Lumpur, Malaysia
CSL Associates
Photo credit: Hideyo Fukuda

3&4
Precima House
Kuala Lumpur, Malaysia
CSL Associates
Photo credit: Jimmy CS Lim

5 Locker Residence
New South Wales, Australia
Harkness Noori Architects
Photo credit: Hisham Noori

6 Neal Residence
New South Wales, Australia
Harkness Noori Architects
Photo credit: Andrew Delaney

7 Belmont Road Residence
Singapore
Consultants Incorporated
Photo credit: Wan Yue Kong, Chew Photo Studio

2

3

4

5

6

7

1

1-4
Connecticut Residence
Connecticut, USA
Elliott + Associates Architects
Photo credit: Hedrich Blessing, Bob Shimer

5 Hooper House
Maryland, USA
Marcel Breuer, Architect
and Herbert Beckhard, Associate
Photo credit: Walter Smalling

2

4

1 **Lipshut Residence**
   Victoria, Australia
   Bochsler and Partners Pty Ltd
   Photo credit: Neil Lorimer

2 **Hamilton House**
   New South Wales, Australia
   Harry Seidler & Associates
   Photo credit: Eric Sierins

3 **House Roberts**
   Pringle Bay Cape, South Africa
   Douglas Roberts Peter Loebenberg Architects
   Photo credit: Geoff Grundling

4 **Lim Residence**
   Singapore
   Alice Lem Design
   Photo credit: Unknown

1

2

3

4

1

2

4

3

5

1 Thom Residence
California, USA
Swatt Architects
Photo credit: Russell Abraham

2 Round Hill Residence
Connecticut, USA
Herbert S. Newman and Partners, PC
Photo credit: Norman McGrath

3-5
West Pennant Hills House
New South Wales, Australia
Woodhead Firth Lee Architects
Photo credit: Adrian Boddy

1 **Fenwick Residence**
California, USA
The Steinberg Group, Architects
Photo credit: Robb Miller

2 **Crocker Residence**
Connecticut, USA
Herbert S. Newman and Partners, PC
Photo credit: Nick Wheeler

3 **Breuer/Robeck House**
Connecticut, USA
Herbert Beckhard Frank Richlan & Associates
Photo credit: Andrew Appell

4 **"Osprey Nest" House**
New York, USA
Herbert Beckhard Frank Richlan & Associates
Photo credit: Andrew Appell

3

1 Bellino-Hall Residence
Oklahoma, USA
Elliott + Associates Architects
Photo credit: Hedrich Blessing, Bob Shimer

2&3
Tootill Beach House
Onemana Beach, New Zealand
Andrews, Scott, Cotton Architects Ltd
Photo credit: Greg Hansen

4 Grand Union Walk
Camden, UK
Nicholas Grimshaw & Partners Ltd.
Photo credit: Jo Reid & John Peck

1

2

3

1

2

3

4

1

1 Pacific Heights Residence
California, USA
Swatt Architects
Photo credit: Alan Weintraub

2 Allen Residence
Victoria, Australia
Richardson Christoff Pty. Ltd. Architects
Photo credit: Max Deliopolous

3 Kumu Honua
Hawaii, USA
Media Five Limited
Photo credit: Images Images, Tim Griffith

4 Raben Residence
California, USA
David Kellen + Associates, Inc.
Photo credit: Images Images, Tim Griffith

2

3

4

1

2

3

4

1-4
Parc Oasis Condo
Jurong East, Singapore
Design Ideas International Group
Photo credit: Albert Lim KS

1 **Elliott Residence**
Oklahoma, USA
Elliott + Associates Architects
Photo credit: Hedrich Blessing, Bob Shimer

2 **Truss Wall House**
Tokyo, Japan
Ushida Findlay Partnership Co., Ltd
Photo credit: Images Images, Tim Griffith

3 **House addition**
Connecticut, USA
DuBose Associates, Inc., Architects
in conjunction with Theurkauf & Co.
Photo credit: Robert Benson

1

3

5

4

6

Dining Spaces

1

Previous
Ong Residence
Singapore
Alice Lem Design
Photo credit: Unknown

1 **Hooper House**
Maryland, USA
Marcel Breuer, Architect
and Herbert Beckhard, Associate
Photo credit: Walter Smalling

2&3
Hamilton House
New South Wales, Australia
Harry Seidler & Associates
Photo credit: Eric Sierins

68

2

3

1

2

3

4

1 **Glendye Court Residence**
   Victoria, Australia
   Holgar & Holgar Architects
   Photo credit: Helen Holgar

2 **Seaside Residence**
   Victoria, Australia
   Nexus Designs Pty Limited
   Photo credit: Neil Lorimer

3 **Como Apartment**
   South Yarra, Victoria, Australia
   Nexus Designs Pty Limited
   Photo credit: Earl Carter

4 **South Yarra Townhouse**
   South Yarra, Victoria, Australia
   Nexus Designs Pty Limited
   Photo credit: Neil Lorimer

2

1-3
St. Georges Road Residence
Victoria, Australia
Holgar & Holgar Architects
Photo credit: Michal Sikorski
(Stockholm)

4 Yu Residence
Talayan Village, Philippines
G & W Architects & Associates
Photo credit: R RL Photography

3

1

1 Lawrence Residence
The Claymore, Singapore
Design Ideas International Group
Photo credit: Xiao Photos

2 Governor's Residence of West Virginia
West Virginia, USA
Dorothy Draper & Co. Inc.
Photo credit: Jaime Ardiles-Arce

3 Belmont Road Residence
Singapore
Consultants Incorporated
Photo credit: Chew Photo Studio, Wan Yue Kong

2

3

Burd Residence
Victoria, Australia
Bochsler and Partners Pty Ltd
Photo credit: Neil Lorimer

1

2

1 **Chiang Residence**
Victoria, Australia
Bochsler and Partners Pty Ltd
Photo credit: Neil Lorimer

2 **Raben Residence**
California, USA
David Kellen + Associates, Inc.
Photo credit: Images Images, Tim Griffith

3 **House Morrison**
Cape Town, South Africa
Douglas Roberts Peter Loebenberg Architects
Photo credit: Laura Jeannes

1

2

1 **Connecticut Residence**
Connecticut, USA
Elliott + Associates Architects
Photo credit: Hedrich Blessing, Bob Shimer

2 **Sophia Court Apartment**
Singapore
KNTA Architects
Photo credit: Tan Hock Beng

3 **House Roberts**
Pringle Bay Cape, South Africa
Douglas Roberts Peter Loebenberg Architects
Photo credit: Geoff Grundling

1

2

1 Truss Wall House
Tokyo, Japan
Ushida Findlay Partnership Co., Ltd
Photo credit: Images Images, Tim Griffith

2&3
  Elliott Residence
  Oklahoma, USA
  Elliott + Associates Architects
  Photo credit: Hedrich Blessing, Bob Shimer

3

Above & Opposite
Grand Union Walk
Camden, UK
Nicholas Grimshaw & Partners Ltd.
Photo credit: Jo Reid & John Peck

2

3

Owner's Suite at the Royal Hawaiian Hotel
Hawaii, USA
Projects International
Photo credit: Rothenborg Pacific

1

2

1

1 Tomewin House
Queensland, Australia
Philip Follent Architects Pty Ltd in association
with Denis Holland - Didec Design
Photo credit: Jane Ulrick

2 Residence at Makepeace
Singapore
Timur Designs
Photo credit: Tim Nolan

2

1   **Foster Residence**
    Victoria, Australia
    Richardson Christoff Pty. Ltd. Architects
    Photo credit: Unknown

2   **Manhattan Apartment, Trump Tower**
    New York, USA
    Dorothy Draper & Co. Inc.
    Photo credit: Feliciano

Dining Spaces   **95**

Kitchen Spaces

1

Opposite and 1 & 2
  Tomewin House
  Queensland, Australia
  Philip Follent Architects Pty Ltd
  in association with
  Denis Holland - Didec Design
  Photo credit: Jane Ulrick

2

Above & Opposite
Tomewin House
Queensland, Australia
Philip Follent Architects Pty Ltd
in association with
Denis Holland - Didec Design
Photo credit: Dick Stringer

1 **Allen Residence**
   Victoria, Australia
   Richardson Christoff Pty. Ltd. Architects
   Photo credit: Max Deliopolous

2 **Talma Building**
   Victoria, Australia
   City of Melbourne,
   Urban Design & Architecture Division
   and Geyer Design Pty Ltd
   Photo credit: City of Melbourne

3 **Noori additions & alterations**
   New South Wales, Australia
   Harkness Noori Architects
   Photo credit: Andrew Delaney

2

3

1 Crittenden House
Victoria, Australia
Bochsler and Partners Pty Ltd
Photo credit: Neil Lorimer

3 "The Townhouse"
Victoria, Australia
Fooks Martin Sandow Pty Ltd
Photo credit: Peter Sandow

2 Bellino-Hall Residence
Oklahoma, USA
Elliott + Associates Architects
Photo credit: Hedrich Blessing, Bob Shimer

4 City House
Victoria, Australia
Cox Architects
Photo credit: Patrick Bingham-Hall

1

2

3

Above & Opposite
House Morrison
Cape Town, South Africa
Douglas Roberts Peter Loebenberg Architects
Photo credit: Laura Jeannes

1

3

4

1

2

1&2
Chiang Residence
Victoria, Australia
Bochsler and Partners Pty Ltd
Photo credit: Neil Lorimer

3 Wartski Residence
Victoria, Australia
Bochsler and Partners Pty Ltd
Photo credit: Neil Lorimer

4 Schwarz Residence
Victoria, Australia
Bochsler and Partners Pty Ltd
Photo credit: Neil Lorimer

3

4

1

2

1

2

Previous
Alderbrook Farm
Massachusetts, USA
Dean Tucker Shaw Inc
Photo credit: Steve Rosenthal

Opposite
House Hasse
Cape Town, South Africa
Douglas Roberts Peter Loebenberg Architects
Photo credit: Geoff Grundling

1&2
Burd Residence
Victoria, Australia
Bochsler and Partners Pty Ltd
Photo credit: Neil Lorimer

1

1-3
West Pennant Hills House
New South Wales, Australia
Woodhead Firth Lee Architects
Photo credit: Adrian Boddy

4   Hamilton House
New South Wales, Australia
Harry Seidler & Associates
Photo credit: Eric Sierins

2

1

2

1 & 2
Fenwick Residence
California, USA
The Steinberg Group, Architects
Photo credit: Robb Miller

3 Belmont Road Residence
Singapore
Consultants Incorporated
Photo credit: Chew Photo Studio, Wan Yue Kong

4 Dillon Residence
Dunedin, New Zealand
Interact Architectural & Design
Services Limited
Photo credit: Gary Van Der Mark

3

4

Opposite & Above
Friedman/Meyer Residence
California, USA
Swatt Architects
Photo credit: Russell Abraham

Previous
  House Hasse
  Cape Town, South Africa
  Douglas Roberts Peter Loebenberg Architects
  Photo credit: Geoff Grundling

Opposite & Above
  House Roberts
  Pringle Bay Cape, South Africa
  Douglas Roberts Peter Loebenberg Architects
  Photo credit: Geoff Grundling

1-3
Marks Residence
Victoria, Australia
Bochsler and Partners Pty Ltd
Photo credit: Neil Lorimer

1

2

Bathroom Spaces

1-3
Belmont Road Residence
Singapore
Consultants Incorporated
Photo credit: Chew Photo Studio, Wan Yue Kong

4 Burd Residence
Victoria, Australia
Bochsler and Partners Pty Ltd
Photo credit: Neil Lorimer

4

1

3

1 & 2
Philips Residence
Victoria, Australia
Bochsler and Partners Pty Ltd
Photo credit: Neil Lorimer

3 Precima House
Kuala Lumpur, Malaysia
CSL Associates
Photo credit: Jimmy CS Lim

4 Residence at Makepeace
Singapore
Timur Designs
Photo credit: Tim Nolan

1 **Johnny Mak Residence**
   Hong Kong
   Alice Lem Design
   Photo credit: Unknown

2 **House Morrison**
   Cape Town, South Africa
   Douglas Roberts Peter Loebenberg
   Architects
   Photo credit: Laura Jeannes

3 **Carson Apartment**
   Victoria, Australia
   Richardson Christoff Pty. Ltd. Architects
   Photo credit: Neil Lorimer

1

3

4

5

1 House Jauhiainen
Espoo, Finland
Jauhiainen CJN Architects
Photo credit: Hannu Männynoksa

2 Lipshut Residence
Victoria, Australia
Bochsler and Partners Pty Ltd
Photo credit: Neil Lorimer

3 Crittenden Residence
Victoria, Australia
Bochsler and Partners Pty Ltd
Photo credit: Neil Lorimer

4 Hamilton House
New South Wales, Australia
Harry Seidler & Associates
Photo credit: Eric Sierins

5 Bellino-Hall Residence
Oklahoma, USA
Elliott + Associates Architects
Photo credit: Hedrich Blessing, Bob Shimer

1   **Chiang Residence**
    Victoria, Australia
    Bochsler and Partners Pty Ltd
    Photo credit: Neil Lorimer

2   **Connecticut Residence**
    Connecticut, USA
    Elliott + Associates Architects
    Photo credit: Hedrich Blessing, Bob Shimer

3   **Chiang Residence**
    Victoria, Australia
    Bochsler and Partners Pty Ltd
    Photo credit: Neil Lorimer

1

2

2

1 **Owner's Suite at the Royal Hawaiian Hotel
Hawaii, USA**
Projects International
Photo credit: Rothenborg Pacific

2 & 3
**St. Georges Road Residence
Victoria, Australia**
Holgar & Holgar Architects
Photo credit: Helen Holgar

3

1

1-3
Marks Residence
Victoria, Australia
Bochsler and Partners Pty Ltd
Photo credit: Neil Lorimer

2

3

1

1&2
Elliott Residence
Oklahoma, USA
Elliott + Associates Architects
Photo credit: Hedrich Blessing, Bob Shimer

3 Irving Road Residence
Victoria, Australia
Holgar & Holgar Architects
Photo credit: Val Foreman

Opposite
House addition and renovation
Connecticut, USA
DuBose Associates, Inc., Architects
in conjunction with Theurkauf & Co.
Photo credit: Robert Benson

2

3

Leisure Spaces

1

2

3

1-3
Douglas Residence
Arizona, USA
Steve Martino & Associates
Photo credit: Steve Martino

Above
Douglas Residence
Arizona, USA
Steve Martino & Associates
Photo credit: Richard Maack

1

2

3

4

1 **Douglas Residence**
Arizona, USA
Steve Martino & Associates
Photo credit: Steve Martino

2 **Douglas Residence**
Arizona, USA
Steve Martino & Associates
Photo credit: Chris Keith

3 **May Residence**
California, USA
The Steinberg Group, Architects
Photo credit: Jane Lidz

4 **Kramer Residence**
Connecticut, USA
Herbert S. Newman and Partners, PC
Photo credit: Nick Wheeler

3

1-3
Simplicity
Mustique St. Vincent and
the Grenadines, West Indies
A.J. Diamond, Donald Schmitt and Company
Photo credit: Images Images, Tim Griffith

4

5

1-3
Arizona Residence - house designed
by Frank Lloyd Wright
Arizona, USA
Steve Martino & Associates
Photo credit: Steve Martino

4 & 5
Villa Nilson
Sweden
Wingårdh & Wingårdh AB
Photo credit: Images Images, Tim Griffith

1

3

5

4

Previous
Villa Nilson
Sweden
Wingårdh & Wingårdh AB
Photo credit: Images Images, Tim Griffith

1 & 2
Tomewin House
Queensland, Australia
Philip Follent Architects Pty Ltd
in association with
Denis Holland - Didec Design
Photo credit: Dick Stringer

3 Tomewin House
Queensland, Australia
Philip Follent Architects Pty Ltd
in association with
Denis Holland - Didec Design
Photo credit: Jane Ulrick

4 - 6
Raben Residence
California, USA
David Kellen + Associates, Inc.
Photo credit: Images Images, Tim Griffith

6

1 **Greenberg Residence**
   Arizona, USA
   Steve Martino & Associates
   Photo credit: Steve Martino

2 **Kangaroo Grounds**
   Victoria, Australia
   Holgar & Holgar Architects
   Photo credit: John Holgar

3 **Hance Residence**
   Victoria, Australia
   Fooks Martin Sandow Pty Ltd
   Photo credit: David Wierzbowski

4 **Dillon Residence**
   Dunedin, New Zealand
   Interact Architectural &
   Design Services Limited
   Photo credit: Gary Van Der Mark

5 **Lansdowne Walk**
   London, UK
   Terry Farrell in collaboration with
   Charles Jencks and Maggie Keswick
   Photo credit: Richard Bryant

4

1

2

3

4

5

6

1

2

1 & 2
   Hamilton House
   New South Wales, Australia
   Harry Seidler & Associates
   Photo credit: Eric Sierins

3 **Burd Residence**
   Victoria, Australia
   Bochsler and Partners Pty Ltd
   Photo credit: Neil Lorimer

4 **Nilly House**
   Kuala Lumpur, Malaysia
   CSL Associates
   Photo credit: Jimmy CS Lim

5 **S Residence**
   Victoria, Australia
   Tract Consultants Pty Ltd
   Photo credit: Graham Barring

6 **Watley Residence**
   Arizona, USA
   Steve Martino & Associates
   Photo credit: Steve Martino

3

4

5

1

2

3

4

5

6

1

2

3

1&2
Parkview Apartments
Tai Tam, Hong Kong
Wong Tung & Partners Ltd
Photo credit: Freeman Wong

3 M House
Petaling Jaya, Malaysia
Pakatan Reka Arkitek
Photo credit: KL NG Photography

4 Ocean House
New South Wales, Australia
Cox Architects
Photo credit: Adrian Boddy

4

1 Ocean House
New South Wales, Australia
Cox Architects
Photo credit: Patrick Bingham-Hall

2 Baan Soi Klang
Bangkok, Thailand
Architects 49 Limited
Photo credit: Architects 49

3 Connecticut Residence
Connecticut, USA
Elliott + Associates Architects
Photo credit: Hedrich Blessing, Bob Shimer

2

3

1 T House
Kuala Lumpur, Malaysia
Pakatan Reka Arkitek
Photo credit: KL NG Photography

2 Lombard Street
California, USA
Swatt Architects
Photo credit: Russell Abraham

3 Neal Residence
New South Wales, Australia
Harkness Noori Architects
Photo credit: Andrew Delaney

4 Precima House
Kuala Lumpur, Malaysia
CSL Associates
Photo credit: Jimmy CS Lim

Opposite
Alderbrook Farm
Massachusetts, USA
Dean Tucker Shaw Inc
Photo credit: Steve Rosenthal

1

2

2

3

Previous
  Conservatory addition
  Connecticut, USA
  DuBose Associates, Inc., Architects
  in conjunction with Theurkauf & Co.
  Photo credit: Robert Benson

1 House Hasse
  Cape Town, South Africa
  Douglas Roberts Peter Loebenberg Architects
  Photo credit: Geoff Grundling

2&3
  Elliott Residence
  Oklahoma, USA
  Elliott + Associates Architects
  Photo credit: Hedrich Blessing, Bob Shimer

Bedroom Spaces

Previous
Owner's Suite at the
Royal Hawaiian Hotel
Hawaii, USA
Projects International
Photo credit: Rothenborg Pacific

1-3
Elliott Residence
Oklahoma, USA
Elliott + Associates Architects
Photo credit: Hedrich Blessing, Bob Shimer

4 Seaside Residence
Victoria, Australia
Nexus Designs Pty Limited
Photo credit: Neil Lorimer

1

3

4

1

1 Sophia Court Apartment
Singapore
KNTA Architects
Photo credit: I.D. Magazine

2&3
Residence at Makepeace
Singapore
Timur Designs
Photo credit: Tim Nolan

2

1

Parc Oasis Condo
Jurong East, Singapore
Design Ideas International Group
Photo credit: Albert Lim KS

3

4

1

1 Doyle Residence
Victoria, Australia
Richardson Christoff Pty. Ltd. Architects
Photo credit: Neil Lorimer

2 St. Georges Road Residence
Victoria, Australia
Holgar & Holgar Architects
Photo credit: Helen Holgar

3 & 4
Belmont Road Residence
Singapore
Consultants Incorporated
Photo credit: Chew Photo Studio, Wan Yue Kong

3

4

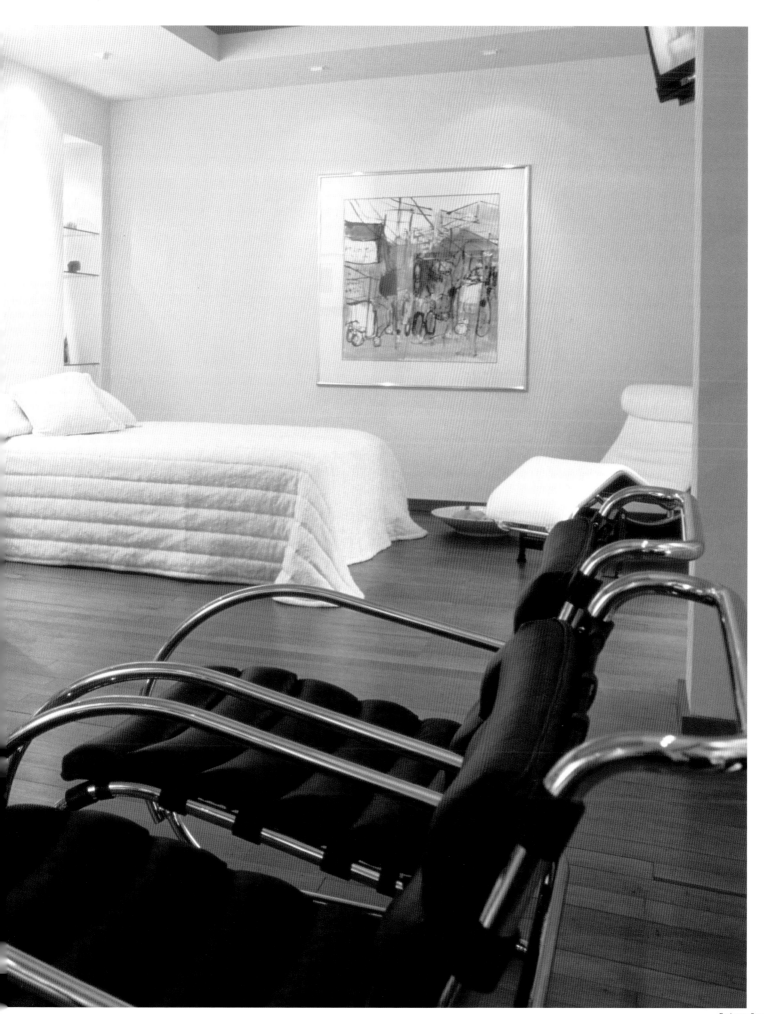

1

Above & Opposite
Tomewin House
Queensland, Australia
Philip Follent Architects Pty Ltd
in association with
Denis Holland - Didec Design
Photo credit: Dick Stringer

1 **Schnyder House**
   Kuala lumpur, Malaysia
   CSL Associates
   Photo credit: Hideyo Fukuda

2 **Johnny Mak Residence**
   Hong Kong
   Alice Lem Design
   Photo credit: Unknown

3 **Vacation House**
   Quebec, Canada
   DuBose Associates, Inc., Architects
   Photo credit: Robert Benson

1

2

1

1 Simplicity
Mustique St. Vincent and
the Grenadines, West Indies
A.J. Diamond, Donald Schmitt and Company
Photo credit: Images Images, Tim Griffith

2 House Roberts
Pringle Bay Cape, South Africa
Douglas Roberts Peter Loebenberg Architects
Photo credit: Geoff Grundling

1

2

1 **Lawrence Residence**
The Claymore, Singapore
Design Ideas International Group
Photo credit: Xiao Photos

2&3
Savannah Residence
Georgia, USA
Dorothy Draper & Co. Inc.
Photo credit: Peter Vitale

3

Courtyard Spaces

1

1

2

1 & 2
Burd Residence
Victoria, Australia
Bochsler and Partners Pty Ltd
Photo credit: Neil Lorimer

3 Simplicity
Mustique St. Vincent and
the Grenadines, West Indies
A.J. Diamond, Donald Schmitt and Company
Photo credit: Images Images, Tim Griffith

1

2

4

1-4
West Pennant Hills House
New South Wales, Australia
Woodhead Firth Lee Architects
Photo credit: Adrian Boddy

5 Kanat Residence
Victoria, Australia
Bochsler and Partners Pty Ltd
Photo credit: Neil Lorimer

3

Above & Opposite
Smorgen House
Victoria, Australia
Cox Architects
Photo credit: Tim Griffith

1

1 **Wong Residence**
 Bin Tong Park, Singapore
 Alfred Wong Partnership
 Photo credit: Alfred Wong

2 & 3
 Tootill Beach House
 Onemana Beach, New Zealand
 Andrews, Scott, Cotton Architects Ltd
 Photo credit: Greg Hansen

2

3

1

1 & 2
Baan Rimtai Saitarn
Mae-Rim Chiang Mai, Thailand
Architects 49 Limited
Photo credit: Architects 49

3 T House
Kuala Lumpur, Malaysia
Pakatan Reka Arkitek
Photo credit: KL NG Photography

4 Yu Residence
Talayan Village, Philippines
G & W Architects & Associates
Photo credit: R RL Photography

3

4

1

1 Belmont Road Residence
Singapore
Consultants Incorporated
Photo credit: Chew Photo Studio, Wan Yue Kong

2-4
Residence at Makepeace
Singapore
Timur Designs
Photo credit: Tim Nolan

2

3

1

2

3

1-3
Irving Road Residence
Victoria, Australia
Holgar & Holgar Architects
Photo credit: Val Foreman

4&5
House Jauhiainen
Espoo, Finland
Jauhiainen CJN Architects
Photo credit: Fotark Oy

4

Opposite & Above
House Roberts
Pringle Bay Cape, South Africa
Douglas Roberts Peter Loebenberg Architects
Photo credit: Geoff Grundling

1

2

3

4

1&2
House Hasse
Cape Town, South Africa
Douglas Roberts Peter Loebenberg Architects
Photo credit: Geoff Grundling

3&4
Crittenden House
Victoria, Australia
Bochsler and Partners Pty Ltd
Photo credit: Neil Lorimer

Opposite and 1-3
Crittenden House
Victoria, Australia
Bochsler and Partners Pty Ltd
Photo credit: Neil Lorimer

Details

**1 Pacific Heights Residence
California, USA**
Swatt Architects
Photo credit: Alan Weintraub

2&3
**Pacific Heights Residence
California, USA**
Swatt Architects
Photo credit: Russell Abraham

**4 Pacific Heights Residence
California, USA**
Swatt Architects
Photo credit: Alan Weintraub

1

2

3

1

2

3

3

4

5

1

2

3

1 **Johnson Miller Residence**
Victoria, Australia
Bochsler and Partners Pty Ltd
Photo credit: Neil Lorimer

2 **Tomewin House**
Queensland, Australia
Philip Follent Architects Pty Ltd in association
with Denis Holland - Didec Design
Photo credit: Jane Ulrick

3 **Schwarz Residence**
Victoria, Australia
Bochsler and Partners Pty Ltd
Photo credit: Neil Lorimer

4 **Preston Residence**
Victoria, Australia
Fooks Martin Sandow Pty Ltd
Photo credit: David Wierzbowski

1 **Boca Bay Residence**
Florida, USA
Burner & Company
Photo credit: Burner & Company

2 **Marks Residence**
Victoria, Australia
Bochsler and Partners Pty Ltd
Photo credit: Neil Lorimer

3&4
House Hasse
Cape Town, South Africa
Douglas Roberts Peter Loebenberg Architects
Photo credit: Geoff Grundling

2

1

3

1

2

3

4

5

6

7

8

9

10

1 House addition and renovation
Connecticut, USA
DuBose Associates, Inc., Architects
in conjunction with Theurkauf & Co.
Photo credit: Robert Benson

2 Hooper House
Maryland, USA
Marcel Breuer, Architect
and Herbert Beckhard, Associate
Photo credit: Walter Smalling

3 Tomewin House
Queensland, Australia
Philip Follent Architects Pty Ltd
in association with
Denis Holland - Didec Design
Photo credit: Jane Ulrick

4 Thom Residence
California, USA
Swatt Architects
Photo credit: Russell Abraham

5 Manhattan Apartment, Trump Tower
New York, USA
Dorothy Draper & Co. Inc.
Photo credit: Feliciano

6 Residence at Makepeace
Singapore
Timur Designs
Photo credit: Tim Nolan

7 Burd Residence
Victoria, Australia
Bochsler and Partners Pty Ltd
Photo credit: Neil Lorimer

8 Smorgen House
Victoria, Australia
Cox Architects
Photo credit: Tim Griffith

9 & 10
Hamilton House
New South Wales, Australia
Harry Seidler & Associates
Photo credit: Eric Sierins

Designers' Biographies

Alfred Wong Partnership

Singapore

Alfred Wong Partnership was founded in 1957, and throughout the period when the evolving economies of Singapore and the neighbouring countries was taking place, the firm developed the capability to produce designs for an extensive range of projects, from schools and industrial buildings to comprehensive commercial developments that include office blocks and hotels.

Reflecting the rapid advancement of the social and economic development of Singapore, the firm has advanced into new areas of specialised building types, such as marinas, and provided design consultancies for "Distripark" projects. These are large scale automated warehousing with a gross floor area of 1.5 million square feet.

While Alfred Wong Partnership currently exports its services, mainly in commercial projects and hotels overseas (e.g. China and Vietnam), the firm is also active in local housing developments. As in the case of all AWP projects, each is specifically designed with respect to the environment, the end user, and towards fulfilling the real needs of the client.

Architects 49 Limited

Bangkok, Thailand

Architects 49 Limited was founded in 1983. It is a firm of professionals offering architectural design services that range from planning, design and production of working drawings, to the coordination and supervision of construction. Through its affiliate, P 49 & Associates Co. Limited, the firm's services also include the design and furnishing of interior spaces. Total services range from the feasibility study through to the completion of the project.

Architects 49 adopts a team approach to its work. At the same time, it requires close and continuous cooperation on the part of the client. Each project, no matter how big or small, deserves full attention from the carefully assigned professional team.

Architects 49 has, from 1989 to 1992, added six affiliated firms, namely 49 Engineering Consultants Limited, A49 Construction Management Limited, Landscape Architects 49 Limited, 49 Graphic & Publications Limited, 49 Model Presentation Studio Limited and Communication 49 Co. Limited, to provide the client with total and integrated services.

These companies, while separately managed, are collectively guided by the same principles which aim to ensure maximum efficiency and optimum benefits for the client.

Bochsler and Partners Pty Ltd

Victoria, Australia

Bochsler and Partners Pty Ltd was established in Melbourne, Australia, in 1980 by Nicholas Bochsler, and is acknowledged by the profession and clients alike for exceptional design capacity at a high level of detail.

The design work demonstrates an assertive individuality, it is characterised by a sense of lightness and openness within which different spaces relate easily with each other. The modulation of geometric forms enclosed by smooth, taut planes belong to the vocabulary of modernist architecture. The spatial experience for the person moving through the building is emphasised. The style is distinctive as is the company's ability to translate clients' needs into excellent architecture.

The ability to undertake and manage the entire project, adding value to the projects by the distinctive design reflecting the quality of the client has been highly appreciated by the corporate clients, who are served by the principals or senior people throughout the project.

The firm embraces a diversity of international backgrounds and experience. The commitment to quality in design, detailing and finishes is evident in the projects, varying in scale, size and type, undertaken by this practice over the past 15 years.

Bollig Abbott Architects

Perth, Australia

Bollig Abbott Architects, founded in Perth, Western Australia, in 1968 offers consulting services in architecture, town and regional planning and interior design.

Managing Director, Dr John Hans Bollig, is an acknowledged leader not only in the business community but in design and townscapes, institutional, commercial and residential buildings and health care facilities. His 35 years of experience is complemented by a group of skilled co-directors and staff members.

The firm has specialists in all facets of building design and management and has made a commitment to create environmentally compatible designs.

Their philosophy embraces energy efficient design standards for commercial and residential buildings. This enables them to produce buildings which not only have distinctive features but have extended investment value and are economical to operate.

They are able to offer decisive aesthetic standards for all architectural work to make the project "stand out" wherever it may be.

Burner & Company

Florida, USA

Burner & Company is an internationally acclaimed, full service, land planning, site planning and landscape architectural firm comprised of innovative design professionals who pride themselves on the sensitive creation of the ultimate exterior environment. The firm has worked extensively on the barrier islands of Florida as well as the Caribbean island of Antiqua, receiving close to thirty state and national awards within the USA; the most treasured being a national Award of Excellence from the American Association of Nurserymen for the North Village at Boca Bay, which was honoured by a White House reception given by First Lady Barbara Bush.

Mr. Peter B. Burner, RLA/ASLA, received his Bachelor of Landscape Architecture degree from the University of Florida at Gainesville, Florida, and has experience in many areas of land use and environmental analysis and planning, site planning and landscape architecture. He currently serves on community development/architectural review boards, has lectured to design students at his university and has been featured in numerous publications for his work.

Ms. Theresa Artuso, A.ASLA, graduated from Rochester Institute of Technology, New York, where she received her degree in Art and Design. Joining Burner & Company at its inception, her creative participation in planning, design and development of architectural and landscape architectural projects incorporates new planning techniques and planting designs which reflect the artist with a living medium.

Design Ideas International Group

Singapore

Design Ideas International is a multi disciplinary design corporation providing services in project management, space planning, interior architecture and interior design, to provide their clients with a comprehensive approach encompassing all of their design disciplines or individual services, depending on the client's needs.

Based in Singapore since 1980, with offices in Malaysia, Indonesia and Hong Kong, Design Ideas International provides interior design services for hotel/resort projects, office buildings, retail and large scale residential projects in South East Asia.

Design Ideas International has a staff of 40 including interior designers, architects, space planners and purchasing agents who are supported by a core of inhouse specialists, skilled in cost estimating, specification writing, documentation research, computer assisted design and development and public relations, allowing them to see projects through from purchasing, construction and installation.

Design Ideas International is large enough to offer a full range of interior design and technical services, yet small enough to offer a very personalised service on your projects. The firm strives to create a unique product, geared to a client's needs bringing its experience and knowledge to every project it undertakes.

Dorothy Draper & Co. Inc.

New York, USA

Founded by Dorothy Draper in the 1920s, the company is the oldest established interior design firm in the United States. Since 1965 the firm has been headed by Carleton Varney, who is associated with the restoration and decoration of countless private residences, hotels and resorts all over the world, including castles in Ireland. He has served as design consultant to the White House and the Carter Presidential Library. He is the Dean of the Carleton Varney School of Art & Design, University of Charleston, West Virginia, and is a syndicated columnist and the author of numerous books on interior design.

The firm has grown to include offices in New York; White Sulphur Springs, West Virginia; St. Croix, US Virgin Islands; and Ireland.

The company continues the tradition of founder Dorothy Draper by being associated with the imaginative use of vibrant colours, floral patterns and bold contrasts.

DuBose Associates, Inc., Architects

Connecticut, USA

Established originally in New York, the firm commenced operations in Hartford in 1958. For over three decades, DuBose Associates has offered a broad range of services in architecture, planning, interior design, space planning and environmental graphics.

The staff of 40 design professionals includes licenced architects and interior designers and specialists in programming, computer aided design, specifications and code compliance. The firm's main facility, located in a historic mansion at 49 Woodland Street, is supported by the latest electronic technology in computer aided design and drafting (20 AutoCad stations, Release 10, 11 and 12), word processing and project management processes for cost control and scheduling.

Recently, the firm's professional efforts have been recognised in design awards by the New England Health Care Design Awards Program, AIA Connecticut, Modern Office Technology and American Woodworking Institute.

Elliott + Associates Architects

Oklahoma, USA

The architecture we create is a three dimensional portrait of our clients. Our projects translate the personality of the leader, or the business philosophy, into an architectural statement.

Established in 1976, the architecture created by Elliott + Associates has received 71 local, regional, national and international awards. Our work has appeared in the following periodicals: *Architectural Record*, USA, *Architecture*, USA, *Designers West*, USA, *Dialect*, Australia, *Interior Design*, UK, *Interior Design*, USA, *Interiors*, USA, *International Design*, USA, *Progressive Architecture*, USA and *Texas Architect*, USA; and the following books: *Architects of the USA*, Australia, *Designing with Ceramics and Stone*, USA, *Empowered Spaces*, USA, *Furniture*, USA, *Graphis Products*, Switzerland and *Interiors*, Australia.

Philip Follent Architects Pty Ltd

Queensland, Australia

Philip Follent Architects - established on Australia's Gold Coast in 1982 - has developed an enviable reputation through a diverse range of architectural commissions. Every project submitted to the Royal Australian Institute of Architects has been presented with an award at local, state or national level including the inaugural Monier/RAIA Australian House Design Commission. Every design is different to suit client needs as well as environmental consideration and no one 'style' is evident. Three objectives, however, are aimed for in every built result: a timeless appeal; an empathy with the site; and the feasibility to accommodate long term changes with relative ease.

Special clients + Good architects = Great architecture.

Fooks Martin Sandow Pty Ltd

Victoria, Australia

Fooks Martin Sandow, Architects is enjoying the 25th anniversary of its founding by being more involved in residential architecture than ever. Although always a cornerstone of the practice, today their work spans from renovations of existing dwellings, new dwellings, both in the project home and custom built sectors, residential interiors to small and large scale, multi unit residential developments.

The practice always works closely with the building owner to develop innovative and distinctive design solutions for each project. The needs and requirements of the client are carefully considered and developed to form the basis of a design brief. The client is consulted at all stages during this process of design development and is encouraged to participate fully during this phase.

The commitment of this practice to high quality is matched by a practical and pragmatic approach to each project from inception to completion of construction within time and cost targets.

G & W Architects & Associates

Manila, Philippines

As leaders in the field of architecture, G & W Architects felt that the only way to effectively address all of the clients' needs for the ideal environment was to focus on both the macro and micro facets of design. Thus the Interior Design Division was born in 1991.

G & W Interior Design Division brings with it more than 25 years of experience in the field of design and execution through its Architectural Division. To date, it has done countless projects ranging from budget condominiums to the plushest of residences; office modular spaces to first class commercial showrooms; pension houses to deluxe and five star hotels. Truly, interior design and interior space planning have come of age in the Philippines, and G & W Interior Design Division is giving a brand new meaning to the concept of the ideal environment.

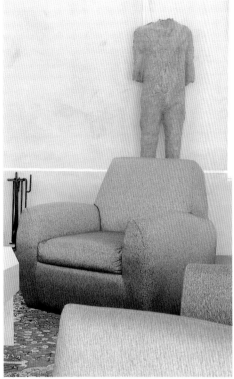

Nicholas Grimshaw & Partners Ltd.

London, UK

After graduating with honours from the Architectural Association School of Architecture, Nick Grimshaw became known for his work in the field of industrial architecture with buildings for such household names as Citroen, Zanussi, Herman Miller and BMW. The Herman Miller building received both the Financial Times Award for Industrial Architecture and an RIBA award. Subsequently the practice of Nicholas Grimshaw & Partners has widened the scope of its work to include sports and leisure complexes, commercial and retail buildings and projects in the field of television and radio.

In 1982 the practice won the Sports Council's national competition for the design of standardised sports halls throughout the UK, with 24 now built.

In 1988 the practice received the major commission for the International Passenger Terminal at Waterloo, and more recently won seven awards, including an award for innovation in the field of Energy Conservation, for the design of the British Pavilion at Expo 92 in Seville.

As well as practising architecture in the UK, France, Germany and the USA, Nicholas Grimshaw & Partners also specialises in industrial design and planning. The practice currently numbers approximately 80 people and operates from offices and studios in Conway Street, Fitzroy Square, London W1.

David Kellen + Associates, Inc.

California, USA

David Kellen has been practising architecture in Los Angeles for over 10 years. After receiving his training at U.C.L.A., Kellen worked for such noteworthy architects as Frank Gehry and Charles Moore. Kellen's designs are bold, but sensitive to the user and the surroundings.

David Kellen, formerly a principal in the firm of Schweitzer-Kellen, designed numerous restaurants and food service facilities including City Restaurant, Gallay, a clothing store, and Juan Juan, a beauty salon.

Some of David Kellen's most recent projects include Rockenwagner restaurant, which appeared in *Interiors*, the Shinko Management Office, which appeared in *Progressive Architecture*, and Monarch Beach Market, which appeared in *Interior Design*. With Jefferson Eliot Concept Design, Inc., David Kellen is part of the team designing a new urban entertainment centre in Singapore. Other current work includes a condominium project in Los Angeles, California, and a house in Malibu, California.

David Kellen's work has been published internationally.

The architectural style of David Kellen is characterised by rich and sculptural compositions where functional and emotional components interact to produce challenging environments that engage participants on many levels.

Herbert S. Newman and Partners, PC

Connecticut, USA

It is the position of the firm that just as it is the task of architecture to provide shelter and accommodate human activity, it is also the task of architecture to dignify and to enlarge the lives of those who experience it. The challenge inherent in each project, after a study of its complexities and its constraints, lies in the search for the concepts and forms that will enable a building to take up a place in its social and cultural context, at once integral and distinctive, as a work of architecture.

Since its founding in 1964, Herbert S. Newman and Partners has applied this philosophy on architectural projects throughout the USA, establishing a national reputation for excellence in design, not only for award winning private residences, but for institutional, corporate and educational clients as well. The work has included campus planning and urban design, new buildings, renovation and adaptive reuse of existing structures, and the restoration of historic landmarks.

Pakatan Reka Arkitek

Kuala Lumpur, Malaysia

Pakatan Reka Arkitek is an architectural firm established in 1979. The firm offers complete architecture, planning and interior design services.

The firm believes in a balanced approach to each project, moulding innovation and enthusiasm with practical experience in order to realise a client's building program and budget to ensure successful design and building solutions. The importance of achieving all critical dates in the design, documentation and contractual process is fully appreciated.

The firm is committed to achieving excellence in professional service and architecture.

The firm's extensive design and practical experience includes office buildings, shopping centres, hotels and leisure buildings, institutional buildings, industrial buildings, apartment and condominium buildings, housing and individual houses.

The firm's work has been published in professional journals such as *Majallah Akitek*, Kuala Lumpur, *UIA International Architect*, London, *Mimar*, Singapore, *RIBA Journal*, London, *Architecture Australia*, Canberra and *A & U*, Tokyo.

Douglas Roberts Peter Loebenberg Architects

Cape Town, South Africa

The partners of the firm met in the late 1960s at Cape Town University, Roberts, the lecturer, and Loebenberg and Moodie, his students. They met again in the 1980s, and the present partnership resulted. By then Roberts had studied in Europe and the USA, and the others had worked in Britain and Europe.

The Cape offers great opportunities with dramatic sites and spectacular views and the firm has built many modern homes in and around the Cape Peninsula which compare with the best of their kind anywhere.

The architect may not always select the furniture for his houses, but his involvement always results in a better product. Of the three examples illustrated in *Residential Spaces of the World*, one is the holiday home of a partner, one the home of close friends of the architect and the third home was furnished by a talented owner who brought his furniture from Europe.

The Steinberg Group

California, USA

The Steinberg Group, Architects, established in 1953, is a 60 person firm with offices in San Jose and Los Angeles, California, USA. The residential practice is extensive, ranging from luxury custom homes, to single family detached, production homes, multi family and senior residential projects. The firm has won numerous national and regional awards for design excellence and has been published in prominent professional journals. The practice also serves civic, educational and commercial clientele. Robert T. Steinberg, AIA, President and Design Principal is a recognised leader in innovative residential design and is a member of the National American Institute of Architects' Housing Committee.

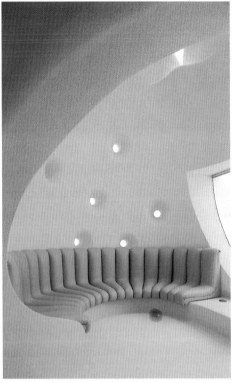

Swatt Architects

California, USA

Founded in 1975 by Robert Swatt, FAIA, to provide comprehensive services in architecture, planning and interior design, Swatt Architects' objective is to create environments that are distinctive, appropriate to their purpose, and reflect a genuine concern for the people who live and work within them.

The firm has a deep appreciation and commitment to both the social and aesthetic aspects of architecture. This commitment can be seen in the beautiful homes designed by Swatt Architects throughout the bay area, which respond sensitively to the user's needs and at the same time are lasting works of art.

Swatt Architects has been recognized with over 25 local, regional and national design awards for single family residences in the bay area and commercial projects throughout the USA.

Ushida Findlay Partnership Co., Ltd.

Tokyo, Japan

Ushida Findlay Partnership Co., Ltd. was established by Eisaku Ushida and Kathryn Findlay in 1986 as a combination of architecture and environmental design. Mr Ushida was born in Tokyo in 1954 and graduated from the University of Tokyo. Ms Findlay was born in Scotland and graduated from the AA School, RIBA. She also undertook post graduate studies at the University of Tokyo and was a Monbusho scholar from 1980 to 1982.

The firm has developed its interdisciplinary activities by viewing architectural phenomena as an accumulation of various experiences and has received many prizes in design competitions.

The firm was reorganised into a company in 1988, and has since been actively engaged in the design of residences, sports clubs, restaurants, recreation facilities, etc. The firm's range of activities also extends into the art sphere, collaborating with many artists.

Wong Tung & Partners Limited

Taikoo Shing, Hong Kong

Wong Tung & Partners, established in Hong Kong in 1963, has been practising under the name of Wong Tung & Partners Limited since 1984. The group is also represented through affiliated practices in Dallas, Atlanta, Georgia, Guam, Canada, Hawaii, Indonesia, Malaysia, Thailand, Shanghai and Shenzhen. The group is associated with the Whisler Patri Architectural Practice in San Francisco in the joint venture company, Whisler Patri/Wong & Tung.

The group is structured to provide a broad base of planning and architectural services which have contributed to a successful completion of variety of projects throughout South East Asia, the USA and the Middle East. It has a total strength of over 200 professional and support personnel. The structure of the group, together with the specialisation of its key personnel, enables the organisation to take advantage of the conditions and special demands of differing projects to create solutions which fulfil both the projects' aesthetic requirements and the clients' needs.

Index

Acknowledgments

IMAGES is pleased to add "Residential Spaces of the World" to its compendium of design and architectural publications.

We wish to thank all participating firms for their valuable contribution to this publication and especially the following firms who provided photographs for the divider pages:

Contents

Dean Tucker Shaw Inc
Alderbrook Farm, Massachusetts, USA
Photo credit: Steve Rosenthal

Living Spaces

Herbert Beckhard, Architect
Beckhard House, New York, USA
Photo credit: Nick Wheeler

Dining Spaces

Richardson Christoff Pty. Ltd. Architects
Foster Residence, Victoria, Australia
Photo credit: Unknown

Kitchen Spaces

Douglas Roberts Peter Loebenberg Architects
House Morrison, Cape Town, South Africa
Photo credit: Laura Jeannes

Bathroom Spaces

Bochsler and Partners Pty Ltd
Philips Residence, Victoria, Australia
Photo credit: Neil Lorimer

Leisure Spaces

Bochsler and Partners Pty Ltd
Burd Residence, Victoria, Australia
Photo credit: Neil Lorimer

Bedroom Spaces

Elliott + Associates Architects
Elliott Residence, Oklahoma, USA
Photo credit: Hedrich Blessing, Bob Shimer

Courtyard Spaces

Timur Designs
Residence at Makepeace, Singapore
Photo credit: Tim Nolan

Details

**Terry Farrell in collaboration
with Charles Jencks and Maggie Keswick**
Lansdowne Walk, London, UK
Photo credit: Richard Bryant